African-American Heroes

Queen Latifah

Stephen Feinstein

Enslow Elementary
an imprint of

Enslow Publishers, Inc.
40 Industrial Road
Box 398
Berkeley Heights, NJ 07922
USA

http://www.enslow.com

Words to Know

Academy Award—A prize for the best performance in a movie.

contract—A legal agreement between two people or groups to do something.

Grammy Award—A prize for the best recorded music.

karate (kah-RAH-tee)—An Asian style of fighting, using kicks and punches.

nominated—Recommended for an honor or award.

theme—A tune; also, the main subject of a song or story.

Enslow Elementary, an imprint of Enslow Publishers, Inc.

Enslow Elementary® is a registered trademark of Enslow Publishers, Inc.

Library of Congress Cataloging-in-Publication Data

Feinstein, Stephen.

    Queen Latifah / Stephen Feinstein.

      p. cm. — (African-American heroes)

    Summary: "Elementary biography of rapper and actress Queen Latifah, discussing her childhood, career in music, and acting"—Provided by publisher.

    Includes index.

    ISBN-13: 978-0-7660-2896-8

    ISBN-10: 0-7660-2896-8

    1. Latifah, Queen—Juvenile literature. 2. Rap musicians—United States—Biography—Juvenile literature. 3. Actresses—United States—Biography—Juvenile literature. I. Title.

ML3930.L178F45 2008

782.421649092—dc22

[B]   2007041550

Printed in the United States of America

10 9 8 7 6 5 4 3 2 1

To Our Readers: We have done our best to make sure all Internet Addresses in this book were active and appropriate when we went to press. However, the author and the publisher have no control over and assume no liability for the material available on those Internet sites or on links to other Web sites. Any comments or suggestions can be sent by e-mail to comments@enslow.com or to the address on the back cover.

♻ Enslow Publishers, Inc., is committed to printing our books on recycled paper. The paper in every book contains 10% to 30% post-consumer waste (PCW). The cover board on the outside of each book contains 100% PCW. Our goal is to do our part to help young people and the environment too!

Illustration Credits: AP/Wide World, pp. 3, 9, 16, 21; Everett Digital Images, pp. 1, 2, 3, 5, 11, 13, 17, 18, 19, 23, back cover; Getty Images, pp. 10, 14, 20; Shutterstock, p. 6.

Cover Illustration: Everett Digital Images.

Contents

Chapter

The Girl With a .... Page **4**
Mind of Her Own

Chapter

Becoming a Rapper .... Page **8**

Chapter

Latifah Becomes .... Page **12**
a "Queen"

Chapter

Queen Latifah Becomes........ Page **14**
a Big Star

Timeline | Learn More | Index
Page **22** | Page **23** | Page **24**

Chapter 1

The Girl With a Mind of Her Own

Dana Elaine Owens, who later took the name of Queen Latifah, was born on March 18, 1970, in Newark, New Jersey. Little Dana was always full of energy. She loved to bang on pots and boxes.

Dana was not interested in the same things as most other girls. Her mother, Rita, often tried to dress her in frilly girls' clothes. But by the end of the day, her clothes were dirty. She lost the bows in her hair.

Dana Owens grew up to become Queen Latifah, a star in music, TV, and movies.

As Dana grew up, she liked karate and basketball, like these kids.

Dana's father, Lance, taught her **karate**. Lance was a police officer. He taught Dana not to be afraid of anything. Dana also loved to play basketball with her older brother, Lance Jr., and his friends.

When Dana was eight, she decided to give herself a new name. Her cousin Sharonda showed Dana a book with a list of names. Dana picked the name Latifah, which means "kind" in Arabic.

Chapter 2

Becoming a Rapper

In 1978, the same year Dana became "Latifah," her parents' marriage ended. Rita and her two children moved into a housing project in a tough neighborhood. In order to support the family, Rita had to take two jobs.

On Sundays, Latifah sang in the church choir. She got good grades in high school. She played basketball and acted in plays. But she wanted to sing more than anything else.

One day, Latifah sang a song in the school talent show. She was afraid people would not like her singing. But the audience liked her so much that they stood up and clapped loudly.

This is Irvington High School in New Jersey, which Latifah attended.

On Saturday nights, Latifah and her friends went to a music club in New York City called Latin Quarters. There they heard rap music. Most of the rappers were men, but there were also some women. Latifah wanted to become a rapper like them. She and her friends Tangy B and Landy D formed a rap group called Ladies Fresh. Before long, they were performing for their friends. Then they won first prize at a school talent show.

Latifah enjoyed performing for an audience.

These are members of the rap group Run-DMC. When Latifah started out, most rappers were men.

Chapter 3

Latifah Becomes a "Queen"

Latifah made new friends who were all interested in rap. One friend, who called himself DJ Mark the 45 King, played records for kids at parties. Latifah and her friends listened to rap music at DJ Mark's house. Latifah worked hard at her own rapping, and she kept getting better.

In 1987, Latifah's friend Ramsey Gbelawoe gave her $700 to make a demo. (A demo is a recording that lets others hear what a musician sounds like.) Latifah recorded two songs in a recording studio. People in the music business who heard Latifah's demo liked it.

In 1988, Latifah signed a **contract** with Tommy Boy Records. Now she wanted a strong name to use for her records and when she performed on stage. She wanted a name that sounded important and would make her feel proud. Latifah decided that she wanted to be called "Queen" Latifah.

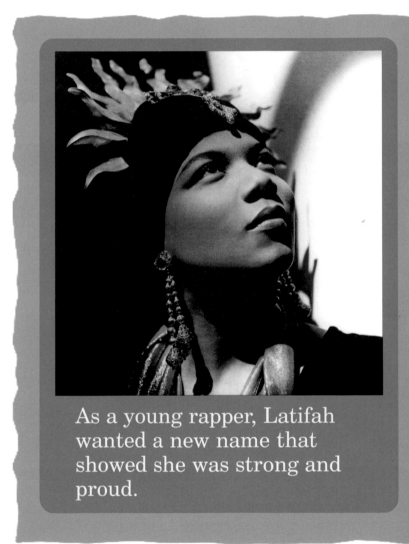

As a young rapper, Latifah wanted a new name that showed she was strong and proud.

Chapter 4

Queen Latifah Becomes a Star

When Queen Latifah's first album, *All Hail the Queen*, came out in 1989, it was a big hit. The album sold more than a million copies. One of the songs on the album was

called "Ladies First." It said that women should respect themselves and they should get respect from others.

The year 1992 started out on a high note for Queen Latifah. She got small parts in several movies. But 1992 turned out to be the hardest year Queen Latifah ever lived through. Her brother Lance Jr. died after being in a motorcycle accident.

Queen Latifah found that the best way to deal with her sadness was through her music. One of the songs on her next album, *Black Reign*, is called "Winki's **Theme**." It is in honor of her brother Lance Jr., who was also called Winki.

In 1993, Queen Latifah began a starring part in the TV series *Living Single*. She also wrote and performed the show's theme music. In 1994, she won a **Grammy Award** for Best Rap Solo Performance for the song "U.N.I.T.Y." From 1999 to 2001, Queen Latifah had her own TV talk show.

The Grammy Award looks like an old-fashioned record player.

Queen Latifah (on left) with the cast of *Living Single*. She was in the TV show from 1993 until 1998.

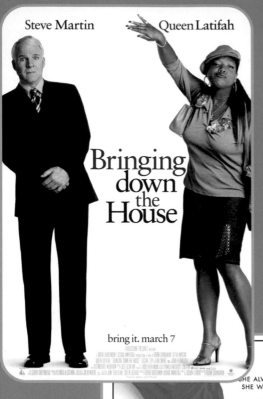

Steve Martin   Queen Latifah

Bringing down the House

bring it. march 7

Hairspray

SHE ALWAYS THOUGHT
SHE WAS SOMEBODY...

AND SHE WAS.

QUEEN LATIFAH

LAST HOLIDAY

COMING SOON

Chicago

Queen Latifah has been in many movies.

Queen Latifah had become a big star. Many more albums, movies, and TV shows followed, including the movie *Last Holiday* in 2006 and the movie *Hairspray* in 2007. She even did the voice for a cartoon. She played Ellie the mammoth in *Ice Age 2: The Meltdown*.

Ice Age 2: The Meltdown

Queen Latifah was **nominated** for an **Academy Award**, an important acting prize. It was for her movie *Chicago* in 2003. She did not win, but she was happy to be nominated.

Two years later, she was given a star on the Hollywood Walk of Fame. This is a famous sidewalk that honors the most popular movie stars.

Queen Latifah with her parents, her sister, Raven, and her brother, Angelo. She is getting a star on Hollywood's Walk of Fame.

Queen Latifah sends strong messages to young people in her rap songs. She tells young girls that each of them has a queen inside. They should feel good about themselves and be proud of who they are.

Queen Latifah's Own Words

"I think I'll never run out of things to accomplish, as long as I'm alive, because there's so much to learn, and so much to do."

Timeline

1970—Dana Elaine Owens is born in Newark, New Jersey, on March 18.

1978—Dana takes the name "Latifah." Dana's parents are divorced.

1987—Latifah makes a demo in a recording studio.

1988—Latifah signs a recording contract with Tommy Boy Records and decides to be called "Queen" Latifah.

1989—Queen Latifah's first album, *All Hail the Queen*, is a big hit.

1992—Queen Latifah gets parts in the movies *Jungle Fever*, *Juice*, and *House Party II*. Her brother Lance Jr. dies after a motorcycle accident.

1993–1998—Queen Latifah stars in the TV show *Living Single*.

1994—Queen Latifah wins a Grammy Award for Best Rap Solo Performance for the song "U.N.I.T.Y."

1999—Queen Latifah has her own TV talk show.

2003—Queen Latifah appears in the movie *Chicago* and is nominated for an Academy Award.

2005—Queen Latifah provides the voice of Ellie the mammoth in the movie *Ice Age 2: The Meltdown*.

2006—Queen Latifah stars in the movie *Last Holiday*.

2007—Queen Latifah appears in the movie *Hairspray*.

Learn More

Books

Payment, Simone. *Queen Latifah*. New York: The Rosen Publishing Group, 2006.

Tracy, Kathleen. *Queen Latifah*. Hockessin, Del.: Mitchell Lane Publishers, 2005.

Web Sites

Queen Latifah's Official Web Site

<http://www.queenlatifah.com>

Internet Movie Data Base

<http://us.imdb.com/name/nm0001451>

Index

Academy Award, 20
All Hail the Queen, 14

Chicago, 20

DJ Mark the 45 King, 12

Gbelawoe, Ramsey, 12
Grammy Award, 16

Hairspray, 19
Hollywood Walk of Fame, 20

Ice Age 2: The Meltdown, 19

Ladies Fresh, 10
Landy D, 10
Last Holiday, 19

Latifah, Queen (Dana Elaine Owens)
    acting career, 15, 16, 19–20
    changing name, 7, 13
    childhood, 4, 7, 8
    rap career, 10, 12–15, 16, 17
Latin Quarters, 10
Living Single, 16

Owens, Lance (father), 7
Owens, Lance Jr. ("Winki"), 7, 15
Owens, Rita (mother), 4, 8

Sharonda (cousin), 7

Tangy B, 10
Tommy Boy Records, 13